by Rex Ruby

Minneapolis, Minnesota

Credits
Cover and title page, © Rosa Frei/Adobe Stock and © africa2008st/Shutterstock; 4–5, © SolStock/iStock; 6, © urfinguss/iStock; 7, © Barou abdennaser/Shutterstock; 8–9, © Westend61 GmbH/Alamy Stock Photo; 11, © /Shutterstock; 12–13, © gary yim/Shutterstock; 14, © Mia2you/Shutterstock; 14–15, © Gabriele Maltinti/Shutterstock and © Peter116/Shutterstock; 16L, © itor/Shutterstock; 16R, © Angel Simon/Shutterstock; 17, © gorillakid435/iStock; 18, © DGHayes/iStock; 18–19, © Matt Anderson Photography/Getty Images; 20, © millaf/Adobe Stock; 20–21, © FamVeld/iStock; 22, © steheap/Adobe Stock, © Mehmet Hilmi Barcin/iStock, © You Touch Pix of EuToch/Shutterstock, © photogal/Shutterstock, and © kearia/Shutterstock; Used Throughout, © Anna/Adobe Stock.

Bearport Publishing Company Product Development Team
President: Jen Jenson; t of Product Development: Spencer Brinker; Managing Editor: Allison Juda; Associate Editor: Naomi Reich; Associate Editor: Tiana Tran; Art Director: Colin O'Dea; Designer: Kim Jones; Designer: Kayla Eggert; Product Development Assistant: Owen Hamlin

STATEMENT ON USAGE OF GENERATIVE ARTIFICIAL INTELLIGENCE
Bearport Publishing remains committed to publishing high-quality nonfiction books. Therefore, we restrict the use of generative AI to ensure accuracy of all text and visual components pertaining to a book's subject. See BearportPublishing.com for details.

Library of Congress Cataloging-in-Publication Data is available at www.loc.gov or upon request from the publisher.

ISBN: 979-8-89232-031-3 (hardcover)
ISBN: 979-8-89232-508-0 (paperback)
ISBN: 979-8-89232-160-0 (ebook)

Copyright © 2025 Bearport Publishing Company. All rights reserved. No part of this publication may be reproduced in whole or in part, stored in any retrieval system, or transmitted in any form or by any means, electronic, mechanical, photocopying, recording, or otherwise, without written permission from the publisher. Bearport Publishing is a division of Chrysalis Education Group.

For more information, write to Bearport Publishing, 5357 Penn Avenue South, Minneapolis, MN 55419.

CONTENTS

So Much Sand. 4
Sand Up Close 6
Crashing Waves. 8
From Mountain to Ocean 10
Freezing and Cracking. 12
Traveling the World 14
Sand from Shells. 16
Green Sand, Black Sand 18
Tiny but Amazing. 20

Science Lab. 22
Glossary 23
Index 24
Read More 24
Learn More Online 24
About the Author 24

SO MUCH SAND

Spending the day on a beach is fun! From building sandcastles to drawing pictures in wet sand, there are so many things you can do! You might even dig your toes into the soft, squishy beach. But have you ever wondered just what those **grains** of sand are?

Every single grain of sand has a different shape.

SAND UP CLOSE

Although beach sand often feels soft, it is actually solid pieces of rock. Looking at sand under a **microscope** helps people see the tiny chunks. These rocky parts might look very different from one another. That's because the grains of sand can come from many different places. They are made of different kinds of rocks.

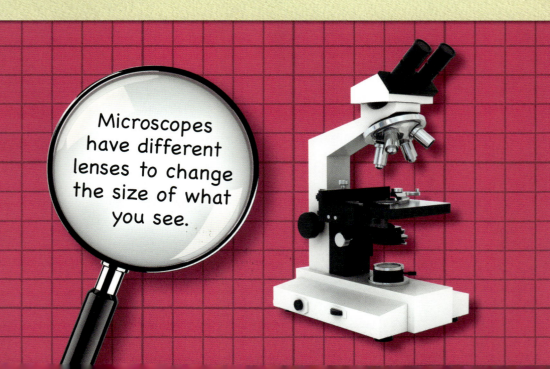

Microscopes have different lenses to change the size of what you see.

Sand under a microscope

Sand grains can feel hard, soft, rough, or even smooth.

CRASHING WAVES

Some sand forms when waves crash against rocky cliffs. Cliffs along the ocean that are hit by powerful waves slowly start to crack and crumble. Tiny pieces of the rocky cliffside fall into the sea and get washed up on the shore. Over time, the grains pile up, forming a sandy beach.

Sand also forms when large rocks break off from cliffs and smash into smaller pieces.

FROM MOUNTAIN TO OCEAN

Sometimes, beach sand starts out on the side of a mountain. When it rains, water flows down and wears away a mountain's rocky **slopes**. Tiny pieces of rock break off and rainwater washes them into a river. Then, the river carries the pieces to the ocean or lake, where they get washed up on a beach as sand.

Beach sand can come from rocky places that may be many miles away.

How Sand Forms from Mountains

- Mountain
- Pieces of rock
- River
- Beach
- Pieces of rock
- Ocean

11

FREEZING AND CRACKING

Changes in weather can sometimes make sand, too. Melted snow may trickle into cracks in rock. If the water freezes and turns to ice, it grows and pushes the cracks open. As the rock splits, tiny pieces start to break off. Melted snow or rain then washes these grains of sand into rivers and out to sea.

Scientists study beach sand to find out what it is made of and where it came from.

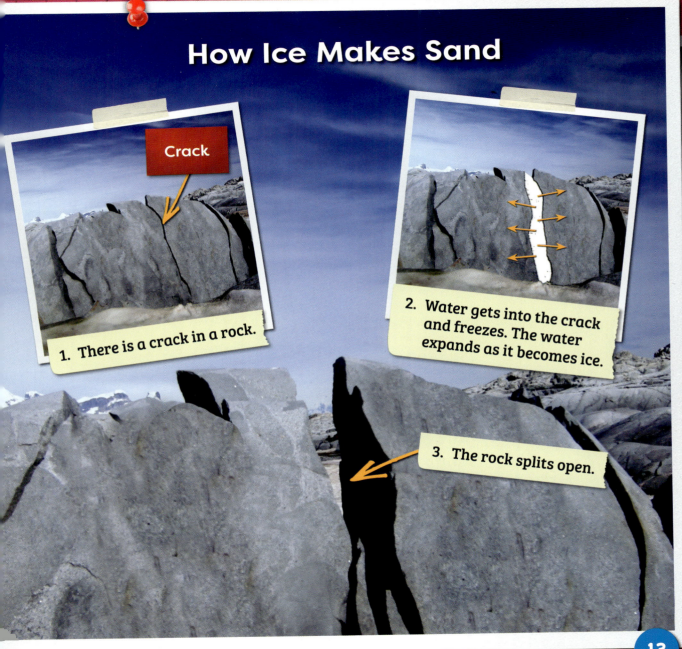

TRAVELING THE WORLD

Wind can send old and new sand on a journey. It picks up loose pieces of sand or dirt. The flying pieces hit larger rocks and new grains of sand break off. When the wind blows across a sandy **desert**, it sometimes picks up pieces of sand and carries them over long distances to a beach.

Sahara desert sand in Africa can sometimes travel more than 5,000 miles (8,000 km) to Florida beaches!

Miami Beach, Florida

SAND FROM SHELLS

Most of the sand on beaches is made up of pieces of rock. However, some sand is made from the **shells** of animals, such as crabs and clams. When these creatures die, their shells get crushed and broken up in the ocean. Then, the tiny pieces of shell wash up on beaches as sand.

Crab shell

Clamshell

The **skeletons** of ocean animals, such as corals and sea urchins, also break into tiny pieces of sand.

GREEN SAND, BLACK SAND

Sand can come in many different colors. That's because sand gets its color from **minerals**. These hard substances that make up rocks are all different. In Hawaii, there is a beach with greenish-brown sand. This sand comes from a rock that contains a green mineral called olivine (AH-luh-veen).

Olivine

Hawaii also has beaches with black sand. This dark sand is made from a rock called basalt (bah-sawlt).

Basalt rock started as lava that came out of a volcano.

TINY BUT AMAZING

The next time you are at a beach, take a closer look at the sand. It might be made from the shells of tiny sea animals. Maybe the tiny sand grains started out as part of a rocky cliff or mountain. You might even be standing on sand that was once part of a faraway desert!

Some beaches even have pale pink sand made from billions of tiny pieces of broken shells.

SCIENCE LAB

Make Some Sand

You can make sand using small rocks, or stones, from a garden or beach.

You will need:
- 10 different rocks or stones
- A metal container with a tight lid, such as a coffee can
- A cup of water
- Coffee filters

1. Place the stones in the container and pour in enough water to cover them. Cover the container tightly with the lid.

2. Next, shake the container 1,000 times! Try splitting the shakes up between friends so you don't get too tired.

3. After you've finished shaking the container, open the lid and remove the stones from the water.

4. Ask a helper to hold a coffee filter over a sink. Slowly pour the water into the filter. It should catch the sand left behind from the bigger rocks.

GLOSSARY

desert a dry place often covered in sand, with few plants and little rainfall

grains small, hard pieces of something

microscope a tool used to see things that are too small to see with the eyes alone

minerals solid substances found in nature that make up rocks

scientists people who study nature and the world

shells hard outer coverings that protect the bodies of some animals, such as clams, mussels, and crabs

skeletons the bones of animals

slopes lines or surfaces with one end higher than the other

INDEX

animals 16–17, 20
beach 4, 6, 8, 10–12, 14, 16, 18–20, 22
cliffs 8–9, 20
desert 14–15, 20
ice 12–13
microscopes 8
minerals 18
mountains 10–11, 20
rainwater 10, 12
rivers 10–12
shells 16, 20
skeletons 17
wind 14

READ MORE

Burgan, Michael. *Rocks and Minerals (Weird But True Know–It–All).* Washington, D.C.: National Geographic Kids, 2022.

McDougal, Anna. *Minerals (Earth's Rocks in Review).* Buffalo, NY: Enslow Publishing, 2024.

LEARN MORE ONLINE

1. Go to **www.factsurfer.com** or scan the QR code below.
2. Enter "**Rockin Sand**" into the search box.
3. Click on the cover of this book to see a list of websites.

ABOUT THE AUTHOR

Rex Ruby lives in Minnesota with his family. He likes going on long walks and discovering new rocks along the trail.